THE GATHERING OF CHAMPIONS

IT'S TIME TO GET IN THE RING

⊷⊶

TRAVIS C. JENNINGS

THE PROPHET'S HOUSE PUBLISHING

ATLANTA • USA • UNITED KINGDOM

A GATHERING OF CHAMPIONS. Copyright© 2009 by Travis C. Jennings. All rights reserved. Printed in the United States of America. No part of this book may be reproduced or transmitted in any form or by any means, electronic or mechanical, including photocopying, recording, or by any information storage and retrieval system, without written permission from the publisher.

    The Prophet's House Publishing
    1450 S. Deshon Road, Lithonia, GA 30058.
    www.theharvesttabernacle.org

Scripture references taken from The Holy Bible: King James Version
"Scripture quotations taken from the New American Standard Bible®,
Copyright © 1960, 1962, 1963, 1968, 1971, 1972, 1973,
1975, 1977, 1995 by The Lockman Foundation
Used by permission." (www.Lockman.org)
"Scripture taken from The Message. Copyright ? 1993, 1994, 1995, 1996, 2000, 2001, 2002. Used by permission of NavPress Publishing Group."

ISBN: 978-0-615-27361-7

Printed in the Unites States of America

DEDICATION

To my lovely wife, Stephanie, my partner for life who has been by my side through tests and through trials…her strong tenacity has brought forth victorious triumph. You have always been the voice of encouragement and the incubator for my dreams. Thank you for pushing me. I love you so much. I will spend a lifetime demonstrating my love for you.

To my precious children, Travis, Briona, Daja, and my little princess Destiny…you have been the inspiration that has fueled me to step out of mediocrity and into greatness. You have encouraged daddy in more ways than you would ever know. My ceiling will be your foundation.

To the church like no other--The Harvest Tabernacle Church. What can I say about this great group of prophetic, powerful, passionate, and progressive people? I have seen you meet challenges, and I have seen you overcome every challenge you have met. I have seen you face obstacles, and I have seen you conquer each obstacle that was placed before you. You are the best. You embody the spirit of a champion. Pastor shares the same sentiments that Apostle Paul stated, "I cease not to make mention of you in my prayers."

ACKNOWLEDGEMENTS

First and foremost, I'd like to thank God for the end-time message that he gave me in this season to minister to his people at a Wednesday night bible study. While I had my message prepared to deliver, the Holy Ghost overwhelmingly invaded my thoughts. I call it "an intrusive prophetic revelation." As a result, he shifted the message to *The Gathering of Champions*. I thank Him for trusting me to carry out this mandate.

I'd like to especially thank a group of people who came together on my behalf to make this book come to be: My wife, Evangelist Stephanie Jennings, Minister Tiffany Cheatham, Deacon Kelsey Hill, Minister Karen Hypolite, Minister Velma Hypolite, Sister Lisa Jackson, Elder Kim King, and Sister Pandreece Reed. Thank you for sacrificing your time with the late nights and many meetings. In addition, thank you also to the Administration team of Minister Shawn Mitchell and Sister Demieta Keener. To the members of the Harvest Tabernacle, you inspire me more than you ever know; you are a church like no other.

Finally, I'd like to thank Jackie Weaver of JW Designs for the beautiful book cover, and the support staff at Lightning Source.

CONTENTS

Introduction	1
Prologue	3
Round 1: Knock Out	5
Round 2: What is A Champion?	12
Round 3: Every Champion Needs A Coach	24
Round 4: Releasing The Champion on The Inside	32
Round 5: Champions Avoid Stinkin' Thinkin'	40
Round 6: The Voice of A Champion	48
Round 7: Every Champion Has Unique Abilities	62
Round 8: Running With Champions	71
Round 9: Every Champion Must First Get In The Ring	78
About the Author	84

In Praise of "The Gathering of Champions"

"In this book, Pastor Jennings teaches that champions do not fight for the victory, but they fight from the place of victory."

Bishop Wiley Jackson
Gospel Tabernacle Church
Atlanta, GA

***

*Peter Drucker once stated, "Every human being has an emotional glass ceiling, a natural resistance to changing identity. Moreover, the ceiling is broken only when the communication is so compelling that it overcomes that resistance." Prophet Travis Jennings in **"The Gathering of Champions"** provides you with a communication so compelling that it will help you breakthrough your emotional glass ceiling, change your identity, and help you to realize that you are a champion.*

This power packed book is a must read for all of us who are striving to overcome our resistance to changing our identity and desiring to make a difference in our world. It will provide you with the principles and core values that champions in any area of life possess. This book will equip you to be a champion in the boxing ring of your life.

Pastor Rodney B. Jackson, MDiv
Gospel Tabernacle Church
Atlanta, GA

***

To the common and the most charismatic, to the average and the highest achiever, to the least and the most successful, and to the peculiar to the most popular, Pastor Travis Jennings, in this book, seeks to motivate all people to pursue the God-ordained champion they were meant to be! He is not just a fighter or a dreamer, but a champion with a cause for other champions. From the ghetto of East Lake Meadows, and from the womb of a 14-year old teenager, was born an anonymous champion, who never thought his bloodline possessed any ounce of fortitude, fight or even a decent future. This is why, with all his might, Pastor Jennings builds his defense for the gather of champions. He calls forth—from the least to the greatest, from the average to the most successful to step in the ring for the greatest fight of their life. He identifies "all people" as champions, encouraging them to tap into a realm of faith in God, which will cause them to reign as champions, just like Jesus Christ. He trains them for battle, employing into all champions the power of God's word. He teaches champions how to avoid the plaques of mental warfare. He motivates champions to combat failure with faith. He admonishes champions to resist the temptation of fear. He shows champions how to use the ammunition of their voice to silence the enemy of defeat. He challenges champions to fight. He coaches champions to win, and he instructs champions to conquer! Don't be defeated—this book is a must read!

Pastor Juandolyn Stokes
Deeper Life in Christ Ministries
Conyers, GA

***

The Gathering of Champions is a "definite must" for the believer who is ready to bring his dream into fruition. It is for those who are ready for the next level in their assignment, and desire direction and wisdom on how to get there. Through his anointed coaching style, Pastor Travis Jennings instructs readers to kick down doors in the mind, break off ungodly strongholds, and arrest negative emotions that prevent them from reaching their fullest potential. With it, he provides life strategies including prayers and confessions that will direct you, placing you on the right path. Prophetically, Pastor Jennings has grasped the key to reaching the common man through his practical teaching approach. He is an expert at "making it plain on the tablets" so that the reader may run with what he has read right into his purpose. His directness stems from his love and compassion to see God's expected end manifested in his people. If you are ready for a change, then you need this book.

Lisa Harrison Jackson
Author, Playwright and Director of *"Hell Is Not a Game Show"*

1 The Gathering of Champions

INTRODUCTION

Over eight years ago I was a struggling pastor in a traditional organization. I was stuck in a rut. All my life, I knew that I was called for greatness, and to make an indelible impression in the earth realm.

My spiritual father once told me, "You have great potential. If you want to fly with eagles you'll have to leave the turkeys alone." Although they both have wings and feathers, the ability of the eagle and turkey are somewhat different. I had to leave the man alone that had my problem and hook up with the man who had my answer.

This is the season for God's people, yet many remain stuck in a rut, watching their lives pass by without ever realizing their purpose or assignment. Many do not grasp the power that they have to change their ordinary, unfulfilled lives ran by the dictates of the world. We live in a world that has told us that we are losers, dumb, stupid, and retarded. According to them, we will never make it.

But I came to give an announcement: This is the season that God's people will have good success. Don't you realize that when you picked up this book, you crossed the threshold? You entered into a gathering of champions.

This process will not be easy. A champion isn't born when everything is good. There will be pitfalls, problems, persecution, and pressure. Every champion has to undergo the process because that is how champions are made. Your spiritual muscles have to be exercised to fight the good fight of faith to win over the attacks of Satan with unwavering stamina and great perseverance. Just as it is when you first start an exercise plan, you will use muscles you have never used before. It's all in the process of preparing you for the big match between success and failure.

As your coach, my job is to motivate you to dream beyond your means, leap beyond limitations, and to achieve astounding acquisitions. Champion, are you ready?

Prologue

It was already a hot, June morning in Atlanta. The sun was beating down, promising a sweltering day like the one before. To escape the stuffiness indoors, residents of the East Lake Meadows community were wandering about the streets in search of a shaded spot to ride out the heat or talk 'junk' with their neighbors.

Among those people was a 14-year-old pregnant girl. Rather than gather with her girlfriends sitting under a shady stoop, she was on a different course. She was restless. Despite her swollen belly, full with child, her only care was to relieve the pain of having to remember how she got into her predicament. She had thoughts of aborting the pregnancy, but she realized that she was too far along. She was pregnant with destiny!

Her baby's father, a 27 year old felon, who was hired as a hit man by notorious drug dealers, was incarcerated yet another time. Because of her rebellion at home, she lacks family support. She thinks she could easily die and be just another statistic in her crime-ridden neighborhood. She feels all alone, but she's not. The champion inside her womb kicks with life, reminding her of every reason why she should live.

Destiny finally arrives! She is unprepared for the birth of her healthy baby boy. Rather than embrace her new state called 'motherhood', she runs away from the responsibility, leaving her baby at the hospital. It is at this point that one would think the story ended, but this is where it really begins.

It was his God-fearing great grandmother who stepped up to claim her great grandson from the hospital and raise him up as she did her own children. The child would be raised in the church and taught the principles of God, including holiness and righteous living. At the age of 14, when his peers were selling drugs, going to jail, or making babies, his life was sold out to Jesus, and he began walking in ministry. If the enemy had his way, the boy would have died in the womb, but God had a purpose for him, a plan, an assignment, and a dream that only he could fill.

How do I know? That boy was me. As you can see, I have been in a place of rejection and abandonment, but God raised me up out of the ashes to do what I was created to do and that was to go into all the world to preach the gospel, bringing forth a prophetic message of deliverance and hope to the nations for such a time as this. I was ordained by God to increase faith and to propel God's people to fulfill their destiny and purpose while walking in righteousness, holiness, and integrity. Yes, me, a little black boy from East Lake Meadows.

So, you see, through God, I am more than qualified to teach you, coach you, and pull you out of your rut and push you into your destiny.

THE KNOCKOUT
FIGHTING FOR THE DREAM
THE FIGHT IS FIXED...

When Martin Luther King Jr. fought against prejudice, racism, and segregation, who would have thought that his speech, "I Have A Dream," would manifest into the likeness of President Barack Obama.

President Obama would have never had this golden opportunity if it were not for past champions such as Dr. King, Harriet Tubman, Benjamin Banneker, Frederick Douglas, Sojourner Truth, George Washington Carver, W.E.B. Dubois, Thurgood Marshall, Malcolm X, Booker T. Washington, Shirley Chisholm, Marcus Garvey, Rosa Parks, and the list goes on. President Obama stands on the shoulders of some extraordinary and grateful giants who have fought the good fight of faith, and now he is laying hold of life and that more abundantly.

CHAMPIONS FIGHT FOR THE DREAM

We know that President Obama didn't come up with this dream by himself. A seed was already planted on the inside of him. Champions know that the Holy Spirit is the dream-giver. He places the dream seed inside of your spirit, but the enemy of your soul wants to abort it. He desires to terminate the dream seed before it becomes mature and reaches the stage of fulfillment.

> *The thief cometh not, but for to steal, and to kill, and to destroy. I am come that they might have life, and that they might have it more abundantly.*
> *John 10:10 [KJV]*

**There is power in the seed!
The enemy is after your dream seed.**

How is the enemy trying to abort the seed? The enemy attempts to abort the seed through parasitic relationships, stigmatic relationships, and democratic relationships.

> 1. **Parasitic Relationships** are those involving people who have the habit of a parasite or leech. These people live off others. They are bloodsuckers and black mailers who rely on others for support and supply.

2. **Stigmatic Relationships** involve a person that is marked and others know it. Because you are with them, you have been labeled also.

3. **Democratic Relationships** are those where decisions are made by voting. Rather than hear from God, you seek the opinions of others.

HOW TO FIGHT FOR THE DREAM

And from the days of John the Baptist until now the kingdom of heaven suffereth violence and the violent take it by force.
                                                              Matthew 11:12

It's important that you protect your destiny by fighting for your dream. As I said earlier, the enemy is after your dream seed. You are going to have to put on strength and fight for your baby like never before. How do you fight for your dream?

1. **Don't curse it, but rehearse it.**

Proverbs 18:21, Death and life are in the power of the tongue: and they that love it shall eat the fruit thereof. [KJV]

You have to see your dream on the canvas of your imagination. God spoke to me years ago about

Ezekiel 37. There God visited Ezekiel in a vision and placed him in a valley of dry bones. The dry bones represented the nation of Israel. Like the bones, they were dry, separate, and lifeless. Ezekiel wasn't literally in a valley of dry bones, but figuratively. He saw the restoration of Israel on the canvas of his imagination. What does that mean? It means visualizing yourself where you want to be in the future. We are what we think ourselves to be.

In the same way, you have to paint your future. Although you're in a hopeless, horrific, or humiliating situation you must still paint your future on the canvas of your imagination.

2. **Don't cry, but release it.**

- Abraham released Isaac back to God
  (Genesis 22:13-14)

- Hannah released Samuel back to God
  (1 Samuel 1:11)

Whatever you are willing to release, God will bring it back in a great measure.

3. **Don't close down, but raise it to the next level through prophetic praise.** Prophetic praise is a new term for the end time church. It is the art of praising God as if it's already done. Praise is a weapon, a tool that should be in the arsenal of the believer to attack the enemy.

Prophetic praise does three things:
- calms the enemy.
- confuses the enemy.
- cancels the enemy's assignment.

CHAMPIONS KNOW THE IMPORTANCE OF A DREAM

The enemy knows the significance of a champion's dream. Because of this, he will try to fight it in every way to prevent manifestation. After all, he knows a dream will:

- cause a nation to increase.
- bring hope to people.
- bless you.
- cause you to laugh.

Champions who possess a dream will encounter three types of people: dream helpers, dream haters, and dream hesitators.

Dream Helpers are those who assist, invest, encourage, inspire, promote, and support your dream. They are the ones who you'd want on your team because they can always be counted on. They are the prayer warriors, the financial backers, and the cheerleaders.

Dream Haters are people who may like you, but not your dream. For them, your dream reveals that they are living life without a dream themselves. Oftentimes, you'd find family members in this category.

Dream Hesitators are the last group. Out of the three groups, people who fall into this category are the most dangerous. Dream hesitators are those who are neutral; they're not for you, yet they're not against you. Because of the lack of commitment, they can hinder your vision.

Now that you know the opponents that you face, its time to gird yourself up to win the fight of your life.

CHAMPIONS MUST UNDERSTAND THAT EVERY DREAM MUST BE TRIED

Joseph was a dreamer. However, his dream had to be tried before he could see the benefits. His journey started in a pit before moving on to Potiphar's house. From there he went to prison before ending up at the palace. Although his journey was difficult, it brought God glory in the end.

Remember that champions always finish strong. Their goal is to annihilate the enemy so that their dreams can come forth. In order to do this, champions must put on their war clothes.

They do this first by knowing who they are. Once they understand that they are a child of the King, they then acknowledge that they need a coach to assist them in tapping into the champion on the inside. Their training will involve avoiding stinkin' thinkin' while recognizing the power of their voice as well as their unique abilities. Finally, champions realize that to keep their environment positive, they must surround themselves with other champions.

It's time to get in the ring and knock the enemy out of the game.

Prayers & Confessions
ଔ ଓ

Greater is He that is in me than he that is in the world.

I have the Greater One in me.

I possess unbelievable power, unbelievable potential, and unbelievable productivity.

The mind that was in Jesus is also in me.

I confess that I'm living out and walking out my God-given potential.

I decree and declare that every hindrance to block my potential has been cast down.

I decree and declare that every hindrance to block my power has been cast down.

I decree and declare that every hindrance to block my productivity has been cast down.

I confess that no weapon formed against my destiny shall prosper.

I release in the atmosphere witty inventions and supernatural manifestations.

I confess that life and death is in the power of my tongue.

I speak life to Power, Potential and Productivity in my life.

In Jesus' Name!

ROUND 2
WHAT IS A CHAMPION?
KNOW WHO YOU ARE

The working definition of a champion is one who fights the good fight of faith, who wins over the attacks of Satan with unwavering stamina and great perseverance. It is a warrior who upholds and defends the integrity of God's word.

Champions do not take "no" for an answer. They don't wait for an open door; they push doors in. Champions know that its war time and as a result, they are always prepared. They are empowered, engineered, and equipped for extraordinary endeavors. How do you know if you are a champion? The following are eight winning characteristics of a champion.

EIGHT WINNING CHARACTERISTICS OF A CHAMPION

1. A champion knows that his life is not his own. A champion empties himself out, so that God can

fill him. When you say yes to God, it is no longer about you. It's about the assignment that he has called you to. In order to fully embrace your assignment, the hindrances blocking your ability to move forth have to be removed.

I am crucified with Christ: nevertheless I live; yet not I, but Christ living in me.
Galatians 2:20 [KJV]

2. A champion understands the power of repentance. He knows that without repentance, iniquity builds in his heart. This blocks the champion from moving forward in his assignment because God is not present.

For godly sorrow worketh repentance to salvation not to be repented of: but the sorrow of the world worketh death.
2 Corinthians 7:10 [KJV]

3. A champion recognizes that meekness is not weakness, but is great strength and unnoticed power.

Five Signs of Meekness
- A champion does not seek his own right.
- A champion is not easily offended.
- A champion never takes revenge.
- A champion is always willing to learn.
- A champion does not try to have his own way.

4. A champion hungers and thirsts after righteousness, while the world seeks money, power, and fame. When you are poor in spirit, your thirst and hunger will never be satisfied. But when your spirit man is strong, God will fill you to the level of your hunger and thirst.

Blessed are they which do hunger and thirst after righteousness; for they shall be filled.
Matthew 5:6 [KJV]

There are worldly sweets that can interfere with your appetite for things of God. The first of these is **synthetic pleasure** as one would find in drugs, alcohol and food addictions. Next there is **soulish pleasure** where soul ties and needy relationships exist. Another worldly sweet is **social pleasure** where the desire to gain social status can be found. Lastly, there is **superficial pleasure**, which consists of a desire for material accumulation. These are designed by the enemy to distract and essentially destroy you.

5. A champion is merciful. He asks the Lord to have mercy on those who offend him.

And he kneeled down, and cried out with a loud voice, Lord; lay not this sin to their charge. And when he had said this, he fell asleep.
Acts 7:60 [KJV]

6. A champion is pure in heart. He purifies his heart daily, so that he can be in right standing with God to enter into His presence.

   Blessed are the pure in heart; for they shall see God.
   Matthew 5:8 [KJV]

7. A champion is a peacemaker. When he evangelizes, he is the bridge between man and God.

   Blessed are the peacemakers; for they shall be called the children of God.
   Matthew 5:9 [KJV]

8. A champion is persecuted for righteousness sake. He is not ignorant of satan's attacks against his mind, body, and destiny.

   Blessed are they which are persecuted for righteousness sake; for theirs is the kingdom of heaven.
   Matthew 5:10 [KJV]

WHAT EVERY CHAMPION SHOULD KNOW

When you hear the title *The Greatest*, there's one name that comes to mind—Muhammad Ali.

The reason why Ali carries that title is because he believed he was *The Greatest*. His belief was so steadfast that he went as far as to let everyone around him know that he was the winner of each of his fights, before setting his foot inside the ring. Because of his confidence, he managed to mentally shakeup his opponents, causing them to also believe this. On the night of the fight, he often turned out to be the winner. Ali didn't allow anyone to dictate who he was or what he was able to do. All he knew was that he was the champ, and he made that known by confessing it at every opportunity.

Like Ali, there is a winner on the inside of you waiting to come out, waiting to break the rope that's been holding you back. If you don't, you will cause yourself to be hooked up to the chain of doubt, fear, and limited thinking. But, there is some good news. God has the best for you. You should dare to do what He has called you to. Even if you experience setbacks, don't give up. Like the old saying goes, "quitters never win, and winners never quit." With Jesus in your corner, you can't lose!

"Ye are of God, little children, and have overcome them: because greater is he that is in you than he that is in the world."

1 John 4:4 [KJV]

That means that there is something greater in you. When you say the word greatest, there's an automatic cap placed on your potential. But greater means a continuous increase or flow. Don't you know that there's some limitless ability in you that is always increasing? You should never stop at one thing, give up on one thing, master one thing, or get bogged down doing one thing, because that one thing is sure to go out of style.

A CHAMPION SHOULD BE OPEN TO LEARN NEW THINGS

To have what you've never had, you must do what you've never done. Do you want to be knowledgeable about finances? Then subscribe to financial magazines and read them regularly. Do you want to learn computers? Why not take a course at a community college?

Many people can't get good jobs, because they are satisfied with doing one thing. This leaves them stuck in mediocrity, looking like Bozo the clown. What they don't realize is that they have a dream inside of them that can't be birthed, because of unresolved issues, unmet needs, and unhealed hurts.

Send a text message to all of the mediocre people in your address book, and tell them that your days of waiting on them to get with the flow are over. Mediocrity gets no attention. Champions don't wait for anyone.

A CHAMPION SHOULD BE READY TO BE DEPLOYED

Champions are proactive and strategic about every move they make. They are the ones who know what it takes to win in every situation. Regardless of the personal issues, setbacks, and disappointments, a soldier remains focused at all times.

Muhammad Ali's trainer, Joe Martin, said that

when he trained Ali as a youth, he knew he was working with a unique individual. Ali was willing to make sacrifices to achieve his dream. He was also determined, and despite the opponents he faced, he could not be discouraged. In essence, he had the mentality of a soldier.

How is God going to deploy us when we are still bound up with different curses? How can He work with us when we are not walking in faith and do not understand our potential? The greater one is on the inside of you. Rather than do things the world's way, soldiers make progress God's way through prayer and fasting. It's time to release the champion on the inside of you, because God is deploying His soldiers.

To build the Kingdom of God, every soldier must be focused on kingdom affairs and not the world's affairs.

No man that warreth entangleth himself with the affairs of this life; that he may please him who hath chosen him to be a soldier.
2 Timothy 2:4 [KJV]

For that to happen, everything must be in order. David is a classic example of a soldier who was out of order. While the kings were at war with the Ammonites, David stayed behind. During this time, he saw and fell in love with Bathsheba. The problem was that she was married to Uriah, a soldier in David's army.

The story continues with David losing his focus and sleeping with Bathsheba which led to an unplanned pregnancy. To hide his sin, he plotted Uriah's death so that he and Bathsheba could marry. As a result, he ended up bringing a curse upon his lineage. Had he gone on to war from the beginning, had he been in place at his post, and kept his focus as a soldier, this never would have happened.

CHAMPIONS UNDERSTAND A FAITH FIGHT

Every challenge that you experience is not a curse, but a faith fight. When you realize that, you'll win over the attacks of satan. Despite the battle, the victory is yours. You might lose the battle, but you won't lose the war. You will declare victory because you are God's champion.

When you are working in faith, you do not care what kind of pain is hitting your head, back, or leg. The head symbolizes your thought process and your creative ability; your back is your stature while your leg represents mobilization. We understand that it is the trick of the enemy to distract us. Therefore, do not give the enemy glory by giving up on what God called you to do.

No weapon that is formed against thee shall prosper.
Isaiah 54:17 [KJV]

EVERY CHAMPION SHOULD KNOW THEIR DESIRED GOAL

Trust in the Lord with all thine heart; and lean not unto thine own understanding.
Proverbs 3:5 [KJV]

Who gave you the goal? God did. If you delight yourself in the Lord, then his desire will become your desire. Champions understand that they did not come up with their goal, but it was God who birthed it out in them. Because of that, he is responsible for bringing it to past. That means you don't have to work for it; you just have to work it. When you come to the dream center, you realize that the goal did not come from your pastor, yourself, nor human ability, but God.

Jeremiah 29:11 says, "For I know the thoughts that I think toward you, saith the Lord, thoughts of peace, and not of evil, to give you an expected end." [KJV]

It was God who put the desire in you. God did it, and that means He's the only one who can satisfy it.

EVERY CHAMPION KNOWS THAT THE VISION IS GOD-INSPIRED.

And the Lord answered me, and said, write the vision, and make it plain upon tables, that he may run that readeth it.
Habakkuk 3:2 [KJV]

The dreams, goals and aspirations that you hold deep in your heart were initiated by God. It is he who gives you the vision.
When you take hold of your vision, three voices will talk to you: the devil, God, and yourself. Your voice always sounds like God, that's why you make mistakes.

- You said, *"The Lord said that's my husband."* But he is not saved.
- You said, *"The Lord said that's my job."* But you frequently miss church, and the stress level is causing you to drink, smoke, and act stupid.
- You said, *"The Lord said, this is my house."* But you are unable to pay tithes because all the money is allocated to the house note.
- You said, *"God called me to preach."* But it has taken you five years.
- You said, *"The Lord told me to lose weight."* But you haven't lost weight yet. Who told you to lose weight? If it was the Lord, why are you not making progress?

When you understand that you need God to give you the goal, then you will effectively accomplish the task at hand.

EVERY CHAMPION HAS TO GET IN THE RING.

In every boxing match, the action doesn't begin until the fighters step inside the ring. Entering the ring represents you starting the game, because the match doesn't officially begin until you take the first step. The hardest step is the first one because it is a step of faith.

The ring is a faith-filled environment. The process of faith can start working on your behalf once you get in the ring. The ring is where you can receive faith to take physical actions.

Action is faith, talking is not. You may have a

multimillion dollar talent inside of you. Telling folk about it is not getting into the ring. You're not doing anything, but wasting your time with haters talking about your vision. You're wasting time with the religious saints that don't want anything in God. Stop sharing your vision with people who aren't going to help you get started. You will face opposition, but remember that the Lord is your strength and salvation.

Take Abraham for instance when the Lord told him the following:

Get thee out of thy country, and from thy kindred, and from thy father's house, unto a land that I will shew thee. And I will make of thee a great nation, and I will bless thee, and make thy name great; and thou shall be a blessing.
Genesis 12: 1-2 [KJV]

In order to see the manifestation of the Lord's promise, Abraham realized that he had to leave what was familiar behind. All he knew was his father and mother, but he chose to take the first step. Every champion needs the gift of 'goodbye' in order to get in the ring.

The grace of God is not released until you first get in the ring. Abraham got in the ring and went to a city he'd never been to before. Don't you want to go somewhere you've never been? Then you must do what you have never done. Now is the time for you to reach your desired goal and the life coach is there to show you the way.

Prayers & Confessions
ఔ ఴ

Life and death are in the power of my tongue.

I decree and declare that my promise will come to pass.

I'm victorious in Christ Jesus. I'm a winner in Christ Jesus. I'm an overcomer in Christ Jesus.

My mind is sharp, my body is fit, and my spirit is alert.

I will accomplish all of what God's called me to accomplish.

I release the spirit of give-up, the spirit of compromise, and the spirit of confusion from my life and those that I love.

When life hurts and dreams fade, I dare to hope again.

I have the ability to dream after experiencing a nightmare.

I confess that I walk in the spirit of perseverance, endurance, and victory.

I shall have whatsoever I say.

In Jesus' Name!

ROUND 3
EVERY CHAMPION NEEDS A COACH

CHAMPIONS CONNECT WITH VISIONARIES

Can you imagine Rocky Balboa without Mickey? How about the Karate Kid without Mr. Miyagi? It's hard to imagine either one of them without their coach. Rocky came in as the underdog in the boxing world, but left a champion, with the help of his coach, Mickey.

There was only one person who could teach the Karate Kid the secrets of the master and that was Mr. Miyagi. Rocky and The Karate Kid, as we know them, would not exist without their coach who pushed them into destiny.

Multiple things happen in life that we don't expect. If you keep on living, you will continue to go through some stuff, but the life coach will be there to walk you through. God wants to upgrade your life. He wants to take you from a place of regular to premium. Every champion has to remove the old, because the old and the new can't stay in the same environment.

Forgetting those things which are behind, and reaching forth unto those things which are before.
Philippians 3:13 [KJV]

God is beating back the clouds, adversity, perversion, and persecution to change the quality of your life.

WHEN THE LIFE COACH COMES, HE BRINGS ABOUT CORRECTION, CHANGE, CONFRONTATION AND CONFORMATION

Champions may experience sickness, failure, pitfalls, betrayals, death, foreclosures, repossessions, divorce, obesity, and/or oppression. On the flip side, they also experience joy, laughter, healing, breakthroughs, peace, salvation, miracles, prosperity, fortitude, birth, and celebrations. The good and the bad are a part of life.

And we know that all things work together for good to them that who love God, to them who are the called according to His purpose.
Romans 8:28 [KJV]

The good, bad, and indifferent are working for your good. The enemy knows how to get you weary in well-doing and tries to beat you at your own game. Aren't you glad that Paul gave us the intelligence? We are not ignorant of the devil's devices.

CHANGING THE QUALITY OF YOUR LIFE

During his short time on this earth, Jesus, the life coach, taught us how to change the quality of our lives.

He overcame frustration, irritation, aggravation, isolation, and intimidation to fulfill His destiny. Let's examine those areas that seem to bring challenge.

A. **Frustration.** Are you frustrated with yourself? Well, maybe you should be. The devil is not to blame for everything that has happened in your life. Things just don't happen haphazardly. We've made some decisions without the Holy Ghost and God's guidance. Consult God next time you make a destiny move.

B. **Irritation.** Are you irritated with people who are holding you back? Drop the dead weight. Let the sapsuckers go, because they are draining your creativity. They might be your color, but not your kind.

Evil communication corrupts good manners.
1 Corinthians 15:33 [KJV]

C. **Aggravation.** Are you aggravated when you know better, but you allow the enemy to win every time? You know that tithing is right, but the devil tells you that a rainy day is coming. You tell yourself that it's ok to keep it, because God understands. Later that day, you become aggravated by the decision that you've made.

D. **Isolation.** Have you ever felt isolated? The devil tells you that everybody else can do it, but you. The devil tells you that everybody else can get that six-figure salary, but you. Stop looking at yourself, and try to see the bigger picture.

Therefore if any man be in Christ, he is a new creature.
2 Corinthians 5:17 [KJV]

E. **Intimidation.** Have you ever been intimidated? Do you compare yourself to others? Be careful, because intimidation can eventually lead to jealousy. If you already deal with intimidation, and you hang out with people who have a little more than you, jealousy can creep in. Appreciate where you are right now. Many people are caught up in the spirit of 'Tomorrow.' They talk so much faith that they get into a vain of not appreciating what they have right now. What if the will of God for your life, at this present time, is where you are right now?

F. **Nauseated.** Are you nauseated with your life? Are you sick of what your life has become? Becoming nauseated is the platform for change. We wanted change in the White House, so we nominated a new president. Once you become nauseated, you will be ready to make a move.

JESUS CHRIST, THE LIFE COACH

Over the years, we have been exposed to the term 'life coach.' A life coach is a professional person who gives strategic plans concerning the course and destiny of our lives. The Lord, Jesus Christ, is the only coach who can give us new life. He is able to transform and revolutionize our lives.

In Him was life, and the life was the light of men.
John 1:4 [KJV]

A champion is not merely breathing, or just existing. Life is dependent on the detail of your living.

He that hath the Son hath life; and he that hath not the Son of God hath not life.
I John 5:12. [KJV]

Every champion needs a coach. When you hook up with Jesus, you will live your best life. He is the only one who can give us new life.

The thief cometh not but for to steal, and to kill, and to destroy. I am come that they might have life, and that they might have it more abundantly.
John 10:10 [KJV]

When the life coach comes in, we must be ready because he brings about **correction**, **change**, **confrontation**, and **conformation**.

A. **Correction.** God has to correct our spirits and our hearts. Life is not based on silent fears, past failures, fantasy in our minds, or perversion in our spirits. Our lives have to be hinged on the word of God. Because of Jesus, we can walk by divine revelation and not physical appearance. Once your spirit has been corrected, you're ready for change.

B. **Change.** God will change your mindset and perception. Champions avoid stinkin' thinkin' by renewing their mind daily with the word of God.

And be not conformed to this world: but be ye transformed by the renewing of your mind that ye may prove what is that good, and acceptable, and perfect will of God.
Romans 12:2 [KJV]

C. **Confrontation.** Every champion has to be confrontational.

But whosoever looketh into the perfect law of liberty, and continueth therein, he being not a forgetful hearer, but a doer of the work, this man shall be blessed in his deed.
James 1:25 [KJV]

A good coach will teach you to always be on the offense and not the defense. He teaches you to take care of a situation before it arises.

You have to confront yourself, if you want to go into destiny and purpose. If you deal with pride, you must confront it. Don't hide it under the rug to collect dust. Pray, fast, and read the word of God to confront every illegal spirit.

D. **Conformation**. After correction, change and confrontation, every champion has to be conformed into the image of Jesus Christ. You have to walk and talk like Him. Every champion's life should exemplify the favor of God and the faithfulness of His people. Focus your attention on Him to be conformed to His image by studying the Bible and obeying His teachings.

Be like Rocky Balboa and The Karate Kid, seize every opportunity to use your coach's wisdom and strategies to defeat your opponent, the devil. Study his every move and don't get caught off guard. Go into every fight with victory in mind.

Prayers & Confessions

I walk in divine favor.

I decree and declare open doors.

I decree and declare opportunities.

I decree and declare chances.

God is making my path straight.

God is leading me into green pastures.

God is surrounding me with favor as a shield.

I have divine connections.

God is sending people to me to affirm, assist, and aid my righteous cause.

I confess that God is raising up people to use their power, their ability, and their influence to help me.

He's removing anyone with bad motives, bad pretense, and bad expectations.

He's eliminating parasitic, democratic, and stigmatic relationships from my life, and He's replacing them with motivators, congratulators, and educators.

He has placed a hedge of protection around me as He did with Job.

I'm releasing people out of my life who cause storms, strife, and stress.

God is connecting me with individuals who sharpen me like iron sharpens iron.

In Jesus' Name!

ROUND 4
RELEASING THE CHAMPION ON THE INSIDE

FROM FIGHTER TO CHAMPION

"Just because you can't see it doesn't mean that it's not there. I want you to embrace that what's on the inside of you is greater than the naked eye can see. You house unlimited possibilities, unbelievable power, unnumbered prosperity, and unusual connections (favor). There is a champion on the inside of you! You have the vision, plans, and the power. The only thing you need is a coach to push you. When we release the champion on the inside, we move into full authority."

~ Pastor Travis Jennings

Every fighter enters a new process of training when he has connected with his coach, and that is the process of releasing the champion from within. The process requires them to confront two realities that ultimately will determine the success or failure of their quest for the prize. It is at this crossroads that the fighter sees two paths.

FAILURE BOULEVARD AND GREATNESS HIGHWAY: THE NEXT EXIT

Failure Boulevard is often crowded with procrastinators, slackers and excuse carriers. These people fall victim to environmental coding and a system that has been designed with the purpose of producing failures. On the other hand, Greatness Highway is wide open with six lanes available to trailblazers, revolutionary thinkers, go-getters, billionaires, dream carriers, and risk takers.

Those who travel this highway are determined to beat the system and dare to walk in champion status. This system was designed and engineered to produce greatness. This system ignores the situations and circumstances of the failing system and calls for an introspection into the power of greatness down on the inside.

...God's [own] handiwork (His workmanship), recreated in Christ Jesus...that we may do those good works...predestined (planned beforehand) for us... that we should walk in them.
Ephesians 2:10 [AMP]

Paul gives us the intelligence that although there is a system designed to produce failure, there is an even greater system designed to launch one from the mundane, ordinary, run-of-the-mill fighter to that level known as **"CHAMPION."**

Ye are of God...and have overcome them (the system of failure): because greater is he (the champion) that is in you; than he [that embraces the worlds system].
1 John 4:4[KJV]

So then, the fighter has to stand looking both paths in the face and make a decision of destiny. Why is it important for these distinctions to be made by the fighter? Don't they have a coach? Yes, but if the fighter doesn't choose to buy-in to the coach's winning system, they'll never be more than a contender.

I AM A PROPHETIC WORD IN PROGRESS.
I HAVE BEEN ENGINEERED FOR GREATNESS.

You will never be able to release the champion on the inside when your life is crowded with internal struggles that you fail to confront. Our society has many former champions that have been brought to destruction because they failed to address demons from their past, their present insecurities, and the doubts of their future.

When you fail to see yourself the way that God sees you, then you will have a distorted, perverse, and twisted view of your life. Your behavior becomes wicked, depraved, and corrupt. To live the abundant life in Christ, you must rid your life of every perverse thought or action.

There are eight prevailing and pestering perversions that must be overpowered and overcome in order to take your rightful place as God's Champion. Let's meet your opponents.

Sexual Perversion
1. Weapons of Choice: Lust manifested in all forms of sexual perversion.
2. Notable Victims: David, Solomon, Absalom, cities of Sodom and Gomorrah, Nabal

Financial Perversion
1. Weapons of Choice: Poverty in the mind
2. Notable Victims: Judas Iscariot, The Rich Young Ruler, Pharisees and Sadducees

Religious Perversion
1. Weapons of Choice: Idolatry promoted by mankind
2. Notable Victims: Pharisees and Sadducees, the Church of Today

Spiritual Perversion
1. Weapons of Choice: Distorting the focus of the spirit of man
2. Notable Victims: Saul the King, Followers of Jim Jones, Christians

Witchcraft
1. Weapons of Choice: A strong manipulation of an individual's mind

2. Notable Victims: Jim Jones, David Koresh (Waco, Texas), Jezebel

Behavioral Perversion
1. Weapons of Choice: Aggression turned inward
2. Notable Victims: The sons of Korah, David, Adam and Eve, Jonah

Family Perversion
1. Weapon of Choice: Attack on the image of the family
2. Notable Victims: Over 50% of all marriages in and out of the church

Perversion of Speech
1. Weapons of Choice: Invades the language and speech of people
2. Notable Victims: Lucifer, Peter, Sanballat and Tobiah against Nehemiah

As you can see, the fighter has a tough line-up of opponents to face in order to reach champion status. The enemy has set these opponents up against those who would dare to leap beyond limitations, dream beyond their means, and achieve astounding acquisitions. This is the lineup you'll face just to get into contention for the belt of victory.

IT'S TIME TO GET YOUR HEAD IN THE GAME!

Champions are overcomers, and overcomers never lose!

1 John 5:4 [KJV] says, for whatsoever is born of God overcometh the world: and this is the victory that overcometh the world, even our faith.

In order to release the champion on the inside you must exercise the "faith force" within you. There is a special, unique untapped anointing on the inside of you.

You are not typical, normal, average, ordinary, regular, general, nor run-of-the-mill. You are super – operating in the supernatural! You are divinity wrapped in humanity. There is *dunamis* (Greek word for extraordinary) power working inside of you. You are a force to be reckoned with. You are a champion!

Champions possess exceptional abilities and powers! When one embraces the "super" that is within him, then he is unstoppable, unshakable, and unmovable. That's why every giant and opponent that's raging in your life is getting ready to come down because you are filled with supernatural power.

THE ANOINTING MAKES THE DIFFERENCE

You are already anointed, chosen by God to be a champion. This is why David was victorious over Goliath.

There are five benefits of being anointed of God:
1. Victories are ensured
2. Demons are destroyed
3. Mountains are removed
4. Sick bodies are healed
5. Atmospheres are changed

Now that you've chosen Greatness Highway, success is inevitable. The champion on the inside of you is yearning to be released. Your destiny is calling you and victory is befalling you. It's time to take on the attitude of a Champion.

Prayers & Confessions

This is the day that the Lord has made, we will rejoice and be glad in it.
I am the head and not the tail.
I will lend and not borrow.
I am above and not beneath.
I am blessed in the city and in the field, blessed when I come and when I go.
Wealth and riches shall be in my house.
I am blessed. My family is blessed.
I'll never be broke another day in my life.
I walk in righteousness, and not condemnation.
I've been forgiven of my sins.
I'm covered by the blood of Jesus and sickness can't penetrate through it.
I'm a son of God.
I'm saved, sanctified, and filled with the Holy Ghost.
I walk in faith, not fear.
I'm a speaking spirit, I have what I say.
I am wonderfully and fearfully made by God.
We are kings and priests unto God.
I live a balanced, healthy, developed life in Christ.
I'm setting a holy standard for my generation.
Favor surrounds me as a shield.
God is able to raise up someone somewhere to use their power, ability, and influence to help me.
I'm a kingdom citizen with benefits from the King.
Even in famine, I will live the abundant life.
Money comes to me NOW!
Healing comes to me NOW!
Peace comes to me NOW!

In Jesus' Name!

ROUND 5
CHAMPIONS AVOID STINKIN' THINKIN'
THE ATTITUDE OF CHAMPIONS

Oftentimes, we complain about the way we have been living, the way we have been loving, and the way we have been giving. If the quality of your life is going to change, then every champion must take a stroll down Transformation Boulevard. It's time to go from existing to excelling, from failure to success, from yesterday to today in order to live the Zoe, which is the God kind of life.

Champions must paint their future on the canvas of their imagination. Champions must understand that God has the ability to change the quality and the fabric of their lives. He's waiting on you to make the mental shift, because your mind has the ability, the capacity, and necessary skills to produce your desired lifestyle. All of the promises of God are received by faith. But God needs your permission and participation to work in your life. God needs you to trust Him and have confidence that everything He promised you will come to pass. Champions become what they think.

For as he thinketh in his heart, so is he: Eat and drink, saith he to thee; but his heart is not with thee.
Proverbs 23:7 [KJV]

Your life is a sum total of your thinking process, and a collection of your thoughts. The way you think creates your reality. The difference between an average man and a billionaire is that most average men run from problems, but a billionaire embraces problems, he solves them and makes money off the outcome. God has engineered you to be a problem solver. Champions at all cost--avoid stinkin' thinkin'.

MIND OVER MATTER

Regardless of the problems, perplexities, and persecutions you face, when the dust settles, a champion is still standing. In a world full of economic devastation, health decay, and family derailment, people are finding it hard to dream, believe, and hope. Companies are downsizing and people are being laid off without warning.

Single parents are the strongest people on earth and now the pressure is harder on them than ever before. They have the responsibility of handling the kids, home and job. You have two parents at home, and according to the latest statistics, only one is working. One person is bearing the load, and the debt is high. Then you have senior people who live on a fixed income. They are dependent on prescription medication, but find it difficult to purchase because they have to juggle its cost with food and other living expenses.

The enemy is trying his best to bring death to our dreams and hope. He knows that the believer has champion power. He knows that he can't kill the potential on the inside. So he paints the portrait of pain, pressure and perplexities. Because of our pitiful present, we fall into a state of depression. Yes, you champion, you overcomer; you believer. You too fall into a state of depression that makes you feel like giving up the fight and letting go of the promises of God.

When you are under this type of emotional stress you're emotionally unstable and mentally imbalanced. As a result, you are placed under suicide watch.

Suicide watch is an intensive monitoring process used to ensure that an individual doesn't commit suicide. Because of pride, we don't want anybody to know that we've been in a dark place, dry place, and a damned (cursed) place. But this book came to interrupt your masquerade party. I'm letting you know that you are not by yourself. Every champion has come through a dry season, a dark season, and a damned season.

If the truth be told the majority of people who fall into this state are believers-- yes the called ones! They are pastors, preachers and prophets. They are psalmists, professors, Ph.ds and professional people. Yes, you have experienced spiritual breakdowns and the enemy is right there to magnify the madness, causing you to feel like God isn't there and his hand it not on your life. The devil is a liar because every champion wins over every attack of the enemy.

In 1 Kings 19 Elijah, the major prophet was battling feelings of:
1. Isolation
2. Alienation
3. Dehydration

His constant battle with the wickedness of Jezebel caused him to fall into a dark place of low self worth, self rejection, and self loathing. Elijah had thoughts of giving up, even thoughts of suicide. He found himself in a dark place--a cave. Yet, even in a dark place, God showed up. Not in a wind, earthquake or fire, but in a soft whisper. No one knows what God told him, but when a believer finds themselves in a dark place only God can pull him out.If you find yourself in a cave of despair, dismalness and depression, I've been raised up at the end time to talk you through it.

EVERY CHAMPION MUST KNOW WHO THEY ARE

But ye are a chosen generation, a royal priesthood, a holy nation, a peculiar people; that ye should shew forth the praises of him who hath called you out of darkness into his marvellous light which in time past were not a people, but are now the people of God: which had not obtained mercy, but now have obtained mercy.
1 Peter 2:9-10 [KJV]

EVERY CHAMPION MUST KNOW WHOSE THEY ARE

For unto us a child is born, unto us a son is given: and the government shall be upon his shoulder: and his name shall be called Wonderful, Counsellor, The mighty God, The everlasting Father, The Prince of Peace.
Isaiah 9:6 [KJV]

EVERY CHAMPION MUST KNOW WHO THEY WILL BECOME

You are a prophetic word in progress. Today's minimum will be tomorrow's maximum. That's who you will become!

Consider what you're carrying. Consider the future generations in your belly that are coming behind you before you give up. Control your thinking. You have the authority to control your mind.

1. **You Must Avoid Stinkin' Thinkin' in Death**
   When your promise seems to have died in your arms, even in death you must control your thinking. When Gehazi asked the Shunamite woman about her son after he died in her lap she responded, "It is well." *2 Kings 4:8-38 [KJV]*. Check your responses. You must recall in your mind what God said. Use the power of recall.

2. **You Must Avoid Stinkin' Thinkin' In Distress**
   Paul controlled his thinking. Even in a distressful situation, he thought himself happy. *Acts 26:2 [KJV]* God's happiness is when one has control over their emotional system and regardless what happens they are aware of His power, they acknowledge His preeminence, and are in awe of His presence. Think yourself happy!

3. **You Must Avoid Stinkin' Thinkin' In Disappointment**
   The woman with the issue of blood went to doctor after doctor with hope that she would be healed, and each time she walked away disappointed.

   And a certain woman, which had an issue of blood twelve years, and had suffered many things of many physicians, and had spent all that she had, and was nothing bettered, but rather grew worse, When she had heard of Jesus, came in the press behind, and touched his garment. For she said, If I may touch but his clothes, I shall be whole. And straightway the fountain of her blood was dried up; and she felt in her body that she was healed of that plague

   Mark 5: 25-29 [KJV]

4. **You Must Avoid Stinking Thinkin' In Delays**
   A blessing delayed is not a blessing denied. In your waiting you're being renewed...you're being built up.

And being not weak in faith, he considered not his own body now dead, when he was about a hundred years old, neither yet the deadness of Sarah's womb: He staggered not at the promise of God through unbelief; but was strong in faith, giving glory to God; And being fully persuaded that, what he had promised, he was able also to perform.
Romans 4:19-21 [KJV]

YOUR LIFE IS A SUM TOTAL OF YOUR THINKING PROCESS & COLLECTIONS OF YOUR THOUGHTS

You are what you think. You are what you are today because of your thinking process. You need to avoid stinkin' thinkin'. The way you think creates your reality. As I said before, the difference between an average man and a billionaire is that most average men run from problems, but a billionaire embraces problems and learns how to solve them.

God has engineered you to solve and handle every problem that you encounter. He has given you everything that pertains to life and godliness according to His divine power. *(2 Peter 1:3)* You need to take a *thought bath*. The word "thinking" in Hebrew means *opens up*. Beware of people filled with fear, doubt, and unbelief.

Prayers & Confessions

I confess that I'm walking by faith and not by sight.

I have corresponding actions to couple my faith.

I confess that God will give me more on my way than when I started.

I don't walk in fear. I don't walk in failure. I don't walk in frustration.

I'm walking in freedom and fulfillment of every promise that God spoke over my life.

The atmosphere that I'm entering is full and conducive for dreamers to birth their assignment.

Every hindering and delaying tactic of the enemy is exposed.

Satan's influences to hinder and to block have been cancelled.

Thanks be unto God that I walk with full assurance that I've won in every area in my life.

In Jesus' Name!

ROUND 6
THE VOICE OF A CHAMPION
LANGUAGE OF CHAMPIONS

Every important vocation in life has its own language. Doctors and nurses, while working in the hospital, have their own language. Firemen and policemen have their language when in the midst of a rescue, dangerous, or life-threatening situations. Pilots and airmen speak the language of the air, and champions speak the language of victory. A Champion does not even know how to speak words of defeat. Rather, champions thinking and speaking line up, they are one. They make sure of this in many ways.

1. **A champion** understands that their words are powerful and what they say will come to pass.

Life and death are in the power of the tongue: and they that love it shall eat the fruit thereof.
Proverbs 18:21 [KJV]

2. **A champion** *never* speaks anything that opposes or is contrary to the truth of God's word. Champions are always conscious and cognizant of what comes out of their mouths!

It's not what goes into the mouth that defiles a man; but what comes out of the mouth, this defiles a man.
Matthew 15:11 [AMP]

Champions can determine their own emotional, social, and physical state through the power of the tongue.

A wholesome tongue is a tree of life: but perverseness therein is a breach in the spirit.
Proverbs 15:4 [KJV]

3. **A champion's** language is life and health; it is impossible for a champion to speak "death talk"…that's not the language of a champion!

Words kill, words give life; they're either poison or fruit— you choose.
Proverbs 18:21 [MSG]

Champions live their life by faith and divine revelation, not by feelings, or physical appearance. It is by the divine revelation of God's Word that a champion moves, lives, and breathes. A true champion is a student of faith who is dedicated to his study and methodology, also known as Faithology. We will explore the meaning of Faithology later in the chapter.

Life is full of adversities, but a true champion consistently confesses the will and the promises of God.

Heaviness in the heart of man maketh it stoop: but a good word maketh it glad.

Proverbs 12:25 [KJV]

Champions never allow heaviness, anxiety, stress, worry, depression, and fear to change the way they talk. Anxiety is an intense fear concerning the threat or possibility of an impending event and self-doubt of your capacity to handle it.

The word stoop means to bend over, or to debase oneself. True champions will not demean or degrade themselves with their own words. The voice of a champion can change your posture in God from being bent over in depression to standing in authority! A real champion can elevate himself with the power of his voice!

WATCH WHAT YOU SAY

Growing up my grandmother would oftentimes tell me, "Son, watch what you say." That statement would come after I've said something that I shouldn't have. In prayer, the Lord told me that the statement was not only a correction, but also a revelation.

This was confirmed in scripture:

God is a spirit: and they that worship him must worship him in spirit and in truth.
John 4:24 [KJV]

And the earth was without form, and void; and darkness was upon the face of the deep. And the Spirit of God said, 'Let there be light' and there was light.
Genesis 1:2-3 [KJV]

In Genesis, God was faced with chaos, emptiness, darkness, and hopelessness. In order to change that situation, He had to say something. He had to find his voice. Both John 4:24 and Genesis 1:2-3 talk about God being a spirit.

In Genesis we find out that God is a speaking spirit. If He is a speaking spirit, and we are made in the likeness and the image of Him, then man is a speaking spirit. We are made of three parts: body, soul and spirit.

When champions are faced with chaos, calamity, and craziness, they are one word away from impacting and transforming their world. Man was created by word in the spirit. Chapter one of Genesis is spirit. God puts the spirit from chapter one into a body in chapter two. Every time God spoke in Genesis, he saw the manifestation of that word. Like our heavenly father, we have decreeing power in our mouths (decree...ordain... establish to make lawful...a rule) God wants us to set the rules in our lives.

So will the words that come out of my mouth not come back empty-handed. They'll do the work I sent them to do; they'll complete the assignment I gave them.
                    Isaiah 55:11 [Message]

So is my word that goes out of my mouth: it will not return to me empty, but will accomplish what I desire and achieve the purpose for which I sent it.
                    Isaiah 55:11 *[NIV]*

In these two versions the word does two things.

1. Accomplishes God's will
2. Prosper

The word that goes out will accomplish the will of the Lord, and it will prosper and complete the assignment that has been sent out. We have been made in the image of God, and His word didn't come back empty-handed in Genesis. We are speaking that same word; therefore, God is going to manifest a word that comes out of your mouth. The word that comes out of a champion's mouth is always victorious.

I believe that in this last day, this end time army of bold, bodacious, brave champions must embrace the power of the spoken word. We have the ability to call those things that are not as if they are.

FAITHOLOGY

Faith is a strong conviction or trust of the invisible causing one to manifest physical actions. Faith is not a feeling. Faith is not revealed to the senses. We have five senses to operate and move through this 3-dimensional world...they are touch, smell, hearing, taste, and sight.

Faith is a sixth sense that works and operates in the realm of the spirit. When one is operating in the sixth sense, they are walking in sixth sense power!

Operating in the spirit means that you believe that what you say will come to pass. Those things that were not, now is, and that all hindrances are removed.

Faith-filled Scriptures

Mark 11:22-23 "And Jesus answering, saith unto them, Have faith in God. For verily I say unto you, that whosoever shall say unto this mountain, Be thou cast into the sea; and shall not doubt in his heart, but shall believe that those things which he saith shall come to pass; he shall have whatsoever he saith. [KJV]

Romans 4:17, "As it is written, I have made thee a father of many nations,) before him whom he believed, even God, who quickened the dead, and calleth those things which be not as though they were." [KJV]

Hebrews 11:30 "By faith the walls of Jericho fell down, after they were compassed about seven days." [KJV]

Faith will make you open up your mouth and confess. Champions call those things that be not as though they already are.

Now faith is the assurance (the confirmation, [a]the title deed) of the things [we] hope for, being the proof of things [we] do not see and the conviction of their reality [faith perceiving as real fact what is not revealed to the senses].

Hebrews 11:1 [AMP]

Faith is trusting in the invisible and believing that what you can't see will work for you. The benefits in trusting God will cause the power of transfer to happen in a champion's life. Faith will cause you to reach into the invisible. What do I mean when I say the invisible? It means the unseen. It is what you're hoping for, praying for, believing for. Faith will cause a divine transfer from the invisible to the visible.

The book of Mark talks about the woman with the issue of blood. She had been hemorrhaging for 12 years. However, she believed that she would be healed. Her healing was in the invisible. It had not manifested yet, but there's a key verse in that particular text.

In the Amplified version verse 28 says, *"for she kept saying within herself. If I may touch but his clothes I shall be made whole."* Listen, the key is that she kept saying, she kept calling those things that weren't as if they were. That's the voice of a champion. Because of that faith, it transferred her healing that was in the invisible over into the visible.

Whatever you need from the Lord, it's already done. It's in the invisible and faith will cause a transfer from the invisible to the visible. To make it plain let's look at the department store layaway plan.

When I was young, my grandmother would take me shopping at a department store downtown. I would see the merchandise and get all excited. My grandmother would make her selections and the sales person would take it off the floor, place it in a bag and put my name on it. From there it went into a warehouse. No, I didn't take it home that same day, but it was mine. My name was placed on the merchandise. I didn't see it. It wasn't in my possession, but it was mine. Every week, my grandmother would hop on the bus, make her way down to that store and put money towards the layaway. One faithful day, when she had paid the layaway off, we were able to take the merchandise that was in the warehouse and transfer it to my house.

Faith is just like layaway. You can believe God for something. It may not manifest right then and there, but if you keep making faith deposits, God's going to take what's in the warehouse and transfer it to your house. That's a good place to praise him!

FAITH PRINCIPLES

Your next blessing will originate from your talk.

Death and life are in the power of the tongue: and they that love it shall eat the fruit thereof.
Proverbs 18:21 [KJV]

People fail to understand the ability of the spoken word. Your next miracle, blessing, deliverance, open door opportunity or second chance is not going to come out of someone else's mouth, but your mouth. The bible says that you should have whatsoever you say. Champions must evict every negative word that is lodged in their mouths, so they can release life and bring about victory and accomplishment to the world.

Your mouth and heart needs to be on one accord with the word of faith.

> *O generation of vipers, how can ye, being evil, speak good things? For out of the abundance of the heart the mouth speaketh.*
> *Matthew 12:34 [KJV]*

Most believers come to church every week. Whether they sing, greet, worship, shout or read the announcements, they are using their voices. Some fail to link their voice with their heart. It's not profitable to only use your mouth in worship, but we also need to connect our hearts with our mouths. Out of the abundance of the heart the mouth speaks.

Meditation is the breeding ground for transformation.

> *Give ear to my words, O LORD, consider my meditation.*
> *Psalm 5:1 [KJV]*

I am an advocate for meditation. I believe the world has stolen the art of meditation. Psalms 1:2 talks about meditation and how it is an undisturbed place that one focuses and concentrates on the word of God. The power of concentration is an undisturbed undivided consciousness that when champions embrace the meditation process, the word that they are meditating on will transform their very lives. They evolve into that word. Growing up, there was a commercial on television with a cartoon character that said, "You are what you eat." In essence, your body is the result of what you eat. If you eat the word, sleep the word, meditate the word, you will evolve into the word that you have eaten. The word says, man shall not live by bread alone, but by every word that proceeded out of the mouth of God.

Your words can and will transform your life!!

Thou shalt make thy prayer unto him, and he shall hear thee, and thou shalt pay thy vows. Thou shalt also decree a thing, and it shall be established unto thee: and the light shall shine upon thy ways.
Job 22:27-30 [KJV]

When I came across these particular scriptures found in Job, my life catapulted to the next level. I discovered that the believer has the power to decree and declare. When champions embrace their ability to decree and declare, they move from the land called ordinary to the palace called extraordinary. In essence, they move into kingship.

FAITH IS A STRONG CONVICTION OR TRUST OF THE INVISIBLE CAUSING ONE TO MANIFEST PHYSICAL ACTIONS

THREE ATTRIBUTES OF THE VOICE OF A CHAMPION

Consciousness

A champion must have a 24-hour, 7-day-a-week consciousness about what is coming out of his mouth.

Consistency

A champion consistently speaks life and has a winner's attitude. Regardless of what is going on, a champion understands that the state of evolution is a gradual change. A champion must understand that your current situation is temporary. You must endure the process!

Commitment

A champion must be committed to remaining conscious and consistent. She understands that she can forfeit the blessings of God by speaking anything that contradicts, counters, or is contrary to the word of God! The voice of a champion must always be consistent with God's voice.

EVEN WHEN YOU ARE DOWN AND OUT, A CHAMPION BUILDS MOMENTUM THROUGH THE POWER OF HIS VOICE!

Even when a champion is down and out, he knows how to build momentum through the power of his voice! When a football team is losing at half-time, the coach builds the momentum of the team by talking...calling those things that be not as though they were.

- Every champ needs a coach. A good coach knows the language of a champion.

Regardless of how Rocky looked (busted lip, swollen eye, and bruised ribs), his coach could look through the eyes of faith and tell him, "It's in the bag, champ!"

- The voice of a coach is crucial to the ear of a champion.

Joshua and the children of Israel released a shout of victory before the wall Jericho came down. They were champions! Jericho was a fortified city. The bible says that Jericho was "straightly shut up: none went out and none came in." But because of the power of their voice, the barriers had to come down!

1. The power of a champion's voice will bring down every stronghold and every barrier in your life. If you decree a thing it shall be established for you.

2. If you speak it, it will manifest.

3. Because you have the voice of a champion, you can speak into nothing and nothing becomes something.

4. Because you have the voice of a champion, you can speak into a dark situation without form and void and light has to appear!

THERE IS POWER IN YOUR VOICE!

Prayers & Confessions

I break all generational curses of pride, rebellion, lust, poverty, witchcraft, idolatry, death, destruction, failure, sickness, infirmity, fear, schizophrenia, and rejection in the name of Jesus.

I command all generational and hereditary spirits operating in my life through curses to be bound and cast out in the name of Jesus.

I command all spirits of hurt, rejection, fear, anger, wrath, sadness, depression, discouragement, grief, bitterness, and unforgiveness to come out of my emotions in the name of Jesus.

I command all spirits of confusion, forgetfulness, mind control, mental illness, double-mindedness, fantasy, pain, pride, and memory recall to come out of my mind in the name of Jesus.

I command all spirits of addiction to come out of my appetite in the name of Jesus.

I command all spirits operating in my head, eyes, mouth, tongue, and throat to come out in the name of Jesus.

I decree and declare that the old man has passed away and I am a new creature on this day.

In Jesus' Name!

ROUND 7
CHAMPIONS HAVE UNIQUE ABILITIES
TAPPING INTO THE REAL YOU

Champions aren't made in the gyms. Champions are made from something they have deep inside them - a desire, a dream, and a vision

Muhammad Ali

In Ephesians 2:10 Paul tells us that we are God's workmanship created for good works, which were predestined and ordained for us to walk in. Every champion must embrace his true identity. The enemy will cause a champion to focus on his identity over his destiny. Your identity is made up of your upbringing, your environment, your tutelage and training.

One walks into their identity through all of those avenues, but destiny is what God predetermined and preordained for you to be, just like he did for Jeremiah. He told Jeremiah I knew you before you were even formed in your mother's womb. He goes on to say that he sanctified him and ordained him to be a prophet unto the nations---now that's Destiny!

Every champion must walk into their destiny because they've been engineered to win! Living in challenging times, many champions might be tempted to compromise, but it's so important for you to look within yourself. You will discover the hardware that God put in you before the foundations of the earth. What he put in you is the unique ability to execute your destiny. Yes, you might look different. You might speak different. Your body structure might be different, but you are uniquely, necessarily, distinctly different for a reason.

As a child, I enjoyed the Christmas story of Rudolph the Red Nosed Reindeer. Rudolph had a unique ability, but because of his difference, no one saw it. He was overlooked. He was left to play reindeer games by himself. But then one foggy Christmas Eve Santa came to say, "Rudolph with your nose so bright, won't you guide my sleigh tonight?" His uniqueness was needed during a challenging time.

Every champion has unique abilities and no two persons are alike. There are special goals, desires, and passions that you have been born with. Great care was given by God to make you into the person you were born to be. But it is up to you to discover, embrace, nurture, and nourish those desires, and passions. Everything that has occurred in your life, from birth to the present is shaping you into your championship status.

Champions must have a desire, a dream and a vision. They can see, smell and taste the victory. There is nothing that will stop them from reaching that goal. These passions drive a champion to get in the ring.

A champion knows that nothing just happens and every loss and every victory is working for your good. That job loss is working for your good. That divorce is working for your good. Being abandoned by your parents is working for your good.

Even in the boxing world, no two fighters' styles are identical. A boxer's style evolves as they apply what they learn in practice, and perform in such a way that turns their efforts into success. Ali once said, "I hated every minute of training, but I said, "Don't quit. Suffer now and live the rest of your life as a champion."

EVERY CHAMP MUST HAVE A PLAN

Every champion must have a plan and a goal for which they are trying to obtain. Because of the goal, the champion's entire life is centered on that goal. *Jeremiah 29:11 states, "I know the thoughts that I think of you, they are of good and not of evil, but to bring you to an expected end."*

From the beginning, God had a goal, a plan, a vision, and a purpose. Despite what happens, it is working for His [God's] good. All things work together for the good. To us it may be bad or ugly, but God says "it's good!"

Let us consider the former heavyweight champion, George Foreman. He was a prolific fighter who was considered a champion at the age of 25. However, he lost to the trash talking Muhammad Ali in a boxing match that he stated left him humiliated to the extent that he quit boxing immediately after the bout. This career shift led him into ministry. Twenty years later, in a tremendous upset and unprecedented event, he won the championship at the age of 45 against Michael Moorer in 1994. Foreman is now considered the champion of marketing his famous George Foreman grill, and other specialty items. A Champion is a champion is a champion.

When you have the heart and soul of a champion, everything that you do will reach champion status. George Foreman invited Christ into his life in the locker room after a brutal fight when the Lord audibly told him to choose Him or choose death. It was then that Foreman committed himself to Christ and laid aside the hatred and anger that used to drive his motivation for fighting. He submitted his training, his skill, and his experience under the cross that beckoned him in the cold locker room.

He started on his own Christian journey and never looked back. Philippians 3:12-14 said it best:

"I'm not saying that I have this all together, that I have it made. But I am well on my way, reaching out for Christ, who has so wondrously reached out for me. Friends, don't get me wrong: By no means do I count myself an expert in all of this, but I've got my eye on the goal, where God is beckoning us onward—to Jesus. I'm off and running and I'm not turning back. [Message]

At one point in Foreman's career, he was called the perfect fighter because of his special qualities. Remember, every champion has a unique ability.

We are fearfully and wonderfully made.
Psalm 139:14 (KJV)

There are no two people, believers, or champions that are alike.

Oh yes, you shaped me first inside, then out; you formed me in my mother's womb. I thank you, High God—you're breathtaking! Body and soul, I am marvelously made! I worship in adoration—what a creation! You know me inside and out, you know every bone in my body; you know exactly how I was made, bit by bit, how I was sculpted from nothing into something. Like an open book, you watched me grow from conception to birth; all the stages of my life were spread out before you, the days of my life all prepared before I'd even lived one day.
Psalm 139:13-16 [Message]

The ABC's Of Discovering Your Unique Abilities

Aspiration
"The Dreamer"

Aspiration is simply the will to succeed. No one wants to fail, feel defeated, or be defeated in any area of their life. The nature of God is to experience the good things in life: peace, joy, love, satisfaction, and the abundant life. Do you have an ambition or dream? Do you have a cherished desire to own your own business, to sing, to dance, write a book, or finish your education?

Every champion must have a desire and a goal for which they are trying to obtain. Because of the goal, the champion's entire life is centered on that goal. *Jeremiah 29:11 states that I know the thoughts that I think of you, they are of good and not of evil, but to bring you to an expected end.* From the beginning, God had a goal, a plan, a vision, and a purpose for your life. Despite what has happened in your life, it is working for your good. *All things work together for the good of them that love the Lord and are called according to his purpose, Romans 8:28.* To us it may be bad or ugly, but God says "it's good!"

Remember if you have not tapped into your personal aspirations, then your life coach is anointed and available to lead you to those hidden goals, desires, talents and dreams. The life coach can assist you in achieving the proper foundation to lead you to personal success.

Basification
"The Transformer"

Basification is the transformation process for a change of position or action. To exceed, there must be change. What are you willing to change in your life to reach your goal, desires or dreams? Are you willing to change your speech, your thoughts and your actions to obtain the desired results?

To get what you've never had, you have to do what you've never done. Live out-of-the-box! Think out-of-the-box! This means that you need new ideas, and a new attitude. *Romans 12:2 says, "Don't become so well-adjusted to your culture that you fit into it without even thinking. Instead, fix your attention on God. You'll be changed from the inside out. Readily recognize what he wants from you, and quickly respond to it. Unlike the culture around you, always dragging you down to its level of immaturity, God brings the best out of you, develops well-formed maturity in you."* (Message).

Connection
"The Handler"

In boxing, a fighter has a trainer or coach who sometimes gets in the ring with him called the "handler." Are you willing to connect to someone who can push you into you destiny? Are you willing to admit that you don't have all the answers, and submit to being trained by your coach?

The handler is the only one who can give you direction for the next level of greatness in your life so that your dreams and desires may be achieved.

When you connect to the coach, you connect to an anointing that will launch and propel you to your place of fulfillment. You were born to do great things; therefore, you must disconnect from anything and anyone that is no longer beneficial to your assignment in life.

Demonstration
"The Illustrator"

Once you embrace the guidance and direction of your handler or coach, there must be a demonstration to manifest your unique abilities. The demonstration of your unique abilities is the evidence or proof that you are a champion. You exemplify every teaching of practical application that your coach gives because you trust in the fact that has already obtained champion status.

As your coach, I believe that your life is an illustration awaiting the next New York Times Bestseller's List. Your confessions in this stage are crucial. It determines your success or failure. You will have whatever you say. Mark 11:23-24 [KJV]

Emulation
"The Winner"

Once you have successfully demonstrated your unique abilities, you should be full of ambition to emulate or achieve what you have been taught by your coach. You are now in the winner's world!

Because you have stepped into the winner's circle, everything in your life is going to increase. Your finances will increase. Your creative ability will increase. It does not matter how big or small your efforts may be, they will always be matched with success because you have trusted the voice of your coach. You are a champion!

> *I am a winner each and every time*
> *I go into the ring*
> *~ George Foreman*

Prayers & Confessions
ରେ ଛେ

I am a speaking spirit.

I am a prophetic word in progress.

When I confess the word of God it will accomplish and bring prosperity.

I can't be defeated. I can't be stopped.

He has caused my enemies to be my footstool.

Because I'm a champion my consciousness, consistency, and commitment to the Kingdom stands firm.

I walk by faith and not by sight.

I walk by divine revelation and not by physical appearance.

In Jesus' Name!

Chapter 8
Champions Run with Other Champions
BEWARE OF THE COMPANY YOU KEEP

In Rocky III, Rocky partners with his former nemesis, Apollo Creed following the death of his beloved mentor, surrogate father, and coach, Mickey. The death of Mickey comes on the heels of a bruiser of a fight brought on by the up and coming fighter, Clubber Lang, portrayed by Mr. T.

Apollo takes Rocky on a personal training course to restore the "eye of the tiger" that once glowed in Rocky's eyes at each fight. There's one scene where Rocky and Apollo are racing full speed down a beach. At first they are running shoulder to shoulder, when suddenly Rocky pulls ahead. He appears to regain his passion, but as they draw nearer to the finish line he begins to fall behind. Flashbacks of his past life with Mickey appear before his eyes, and he slows to a jog before giving up altogether. At the end, Apollo wins the race and runs back to Rocky screaming, "What's the matter with you?"

When you are running with champions, your

environment is crucial. In Rocky's case his environment was in his mind. He couldn't think past the death of Mickey. Mickey's passing took him off guard, stripping him of his self worth, and his will to move into destiny. In his mind, Mickey was the only one who shared his passion for boxing. Although Apollo was also a boxer, they didn't have the same relationship. As a result, Rocky was willing to let a dream die. When he looked in the mirror, he couldn't see what Apollo saw. He didn't think he was the champ any longer.

Two unlike things can't function together unless they are on the same level. That is why you will never see cats and dogs running together. That's why when you see pine trees; you normally see other pine trees not maple trees. Turkeys and eagles don't hang out together. One can't get beyond the barnyard and the other won't leave his perch high in the sky.

In Jonah the first chapter, God told Jonah to arise and go to Nineveh that great city and cry against it for their wickedness. But Jonah disobeyed and went to Tarshish which is opposite of Nineveh from the presence of the Lord.

Because of his disobedience, God sent a great wind that tossed the ship almost to the breaking point. The men cried to their own gods for help and threw the cargo overboard to lighten the ship. Then the Captain went down to where Jonah was sleeping and said, "Jonah cry to your God that we might be spared." Now how did they know Jonah served Jehovah God?

Then they said, "come now let us cast lots that we may know for whose cause this evil has come on us." The lots fell upon Jonah. And Jonah answered them and said, "I am a Hebrew, and I fear the Lord which has made the heavens, the sea and the dry land." Then the men were afraid of him and ask him, "Why have you done this?" The men knew that he had fled from the presence of God because he told them. So they took Jonah and cast him overboard and the sea stopped its raging.

HAVING THE WRONG PERSON WITH YOU CAN CAUSE YOU TO GO THROUGH STORMS, STRESS AND STRIFE.

If you are going to be a champion who fights the good fight of faith and wins over the attacks of Satan with unwavering stamina and great perseverance, then you have to watch the company you keep. Who you are connected to has everything to do with how you come out in the end.

Don't be deceived, evil communication corrupts good manners.
1 Corinthians 15:33

Don't you know that the antonym for champion is loser? Now is not the time to be hooked up with losers. It is time to get rid of all the losers on your boat! They will drain all of your creativity and consecration. They don't want anything, and they don't want you to have anything.

Jonah was running from God. The men did not ask for the storm to come, they just had the wrong person in the boat. When you think of a loser, you might think of someone that you don't like or don't know, but they can come in different forms. They can be a church member, family member, or a co-worker. Whoever it is, you must throw them overboard if you want the storm winds to cease.

God is tired of you going through trouble because of someone else.

WRONG PEOPLE KEEP YOU IN A STRESSFUL ENVIRONMENT.

Nothing is peaceful when you're connected to the wrong people. Aren't you tired of doing business with people who are not on your same wave length? You are soaring high like an eagle in God, while they are still squabbling down there with the pigeons.

You know those people. Every time you're in their presence you can't relax. You're not yourself; you must watch what you say, or what you do. You're always on edge because you do not want to frustrate them. But today that's over. Zion is calling you to a higher place of praise, and you're running with champions. From this moment forward, throw every Jonah overboard.

So we know thus far that running with the wrong people can cause storms and stress, but it can also cause strife. Strife is another way of saying conflict. Every time you're in the company of the wrong people, sometimes you find yourself angry when you leave their presence. That's a clear sign that Jonah is on the ship. Your heart is not pure, because you let an unsanctified Jonah in your life.

Now you have anger and bitterness in your spirit, because you've allowed Jonah to come on board. You must leave the loser alone, and hook up with the man who has your answer. When you run with champions, you'll realize that you can no longer entertain mediocrity. You can't think the way others think. Yet at the same time, you understand that you need the right connections to propel you to a place of fulfillment.

RUNNING WITH CHAMPIONS WILL CAUSE ONE TO BE TAILORED.

Iron sharpens iron; so a man sharpens the countenance of his friend.
Proverbs 27:17 [AMP]

Everything you need is already in you, but you need some scissors in the Holy Ghost. You need somebody to cut on you and tailor you. You may have a gift of prophesy, or preaching may be your calling, but you need to sit under a man of God that can tailor you for your best fit. As you read these words, you're being tailored. Snip, snip, snip---shift. Your season just changed, and Jonah has left your boat. Your glory is increasing, because you are now running with champions.

CHAMPIONS HANG OUT TOGETHER BECAUSE YOUR NETWORK DETERMINES YOUR NET WORTH.

In the Verizon commercials, a man is seen walking in precarious places with confidence because he knows that no matter where he goes, his network has his back. His signal is strengthened, because of his network. He knows that he won't lose. Your network determines your net worth. Evaluate your network. If anyone causes the value of your network to decline, you must let them go. God is re-arranging your network because you are destined for greatness. Your network can't hold you back, but must back you up.

Deep down, you know there is a champion inside of you. There is a hunger inside of your soul for purpose. God has been shaking you to the point that you cannot sleep at night. There is something inside of your heart that you cannot contain, and you need more of His power. You don't need more houses, or cars or money, you need more of God. You know that God is calling you higher. Seek Him and His righteousness and all these things shall be added unto you.

At the end of the movie, Rocky came around and he went on to beat Clubber Lang in a rematch. What would have happened if he decided not to agree with Apollo and threw in the towel early on? He wouldn't have retained his championship status. When you are a champion, you need other champions to encourage and support you. Remember your network determines your net worth. Champions only run with other champions. Now ask yourself, who are you running with these days?

Prayers & Confessions

I decree and declare that because of my connection with you Lord, I will walk into a level of fulfillment.

I decree and declare that because of my connection, I will move prophetically by calling those things that be not as though they were.

I decree and declare that because of my connection, my family's assignment is one that reflects the Kingdom of God.

I decree and declare that because of my connection, your wisdom is upon me and causes astounding acquisitions.

I decree and declare that because of my connection, that any form of curse, witchcraft, sorcery, evil powers, soul ties, occult affiliations, immoral acts are destroyed in the name of Jesus!

I decree and declare that because of my connection, the blood of Jesus covers me and sickness and disease can't penetrate through it.

I decree and declare that because of my connection, your favor causes supernatural increase, supernatural harvest, and supernatural grace to be upon me.

I decree and declare that because of my connection, my faith will always under all circumstances, cause me to walk in victory.

In Jesus' Name!

ROUND 9
CHAMPIONS GET IN THE RING
LET'S GET READY TO RUMBLE!

Are you tired of the merry-go-round? Are you tired of life passing you by, people passing you by, and dreams fading away? Have you ever said to yourself, 'enough is enough, and too much is too much?' How about, 'I can't take this anymore.' Or, 'Why was I even born?'

Satan desires to keep you outside the ring. He throws punches of confusion, doubt, fear, and self-inflicted pain to destroy your life. Why? Because when you're outside of the ring, destiny and purpose are not an option—they don't exist in that state. Outside the ring you are not in a qualified match, you are street fighting and with street fighting there are no rules. When you're outside the ring you aren't fighting for anything.

You are literally beating at the air because you don't know who you are, whose you are and what you're fighting for. When you know who you are, you become a threat to the enemy.

The ring is a place of possibilities, a place of perseverance, it is the battleground and battlefield; a place where battles are lost and victories are won. The ring's atmosphere is conducive for manifestation.

It's only in the ring where dreams and visions come forth. God gives witty inventions and ideas in the ring. Your book is in the ring. The next level of your marriage is in the ring. Pastors, your church building is in the ring. God gives supernatural intelligence to you whereas it would be harder for others.

The enemy knows that the ring's atmosphere is conducive for dreamers to birth. Once you enter the ring you are no longer in satan's territory. He can't hit below the belt, hold, trip, kick, head butt, wrestle, or push you anymore. Champions use whatever tactic is necessary to destroy the enemy. Mobilization is a must.

WHAT STOPS MOBILIZATION?

1. **All Talk and No Walk**

   Many people have great expectations, even glorious revelations, but they lack mobilization. When people can't get moving, they say things like: *"I'm going to," "I'm putting things in order," "I will one day,"* or *"If the Lord is willing."*

   James 2:17 says, Isn't it obvious that God-talk without God-acts is outrageous nonsense? [Msg]

2. **Mistaking Fantasy with Faith**
   Many Christians live mediocre lives because of defective judgment, deficient knowledge, or

carelessness, mistaking fantasy with faith.

Hosea 4:6 [KJV] says; my people are destroyed for lack of knowledge.

Fantasy causes one to become self indulgent and caught up in their self-willed desires, self-gain, and keeps them outside the will of God. For this reason you must wake up out of fantasy land! Fantasy is your imagination gone wild absent from reality. Faith on the other hand is a strong conviction or trust of the invisible causing one to manifest physical actions

3. Finances with no Freedom

God never intended for your finances to be held hostage to situations and circumstances. Life has caused many to have a warped and distorted view about finances and this stops mobilization. Your finances must have freedom to travel and fund God-inspired projects.

2 Corinthians 9:8 [AMP] says, And God is able to make all grace (every favor and earthly blessing) come to you in abundance, so that you may always and under all circumstances and whatever the need be self-sufficient [possessing enough to require no aid or support and furnished in abundance for every good work and charitable donation].

Champions know that faith can do what finances can't.

4. Family Full of Fools

Family is the biggest hindrance to promotion and mobilization. At times they can appear to be evil outlaws and ego-maniacs, entrapping you in past failures, past pain, and past relationships. Because of emotional soul ties, you entertain familiar spirits disguised as family reunions at Big Mamma's house. Stop the madness and take a look at your family scroll. What spirits are common in your family? Champions don't let familiar spirits rule their lives.

5. Fear of Fulfillment

<u>Fear Permeates</u>
Fear gets down into the core of the individual that is ruled by it. They talk, walk, sneeze, cough, and eat fear. *Matthew 12:34 [KJV] For out of the abundance of the heart the mouth speaks.* Don't let fear cause your mouth to curse your destiny.

<u>Fear Parades</u>
Your opponent can look at you and see fear on your face. Don't allow fear to flaunt you around ostentatiously and deprive your life of future glory. Cease immediately from letting the enemy make you cry, as a matter of fact, don't even let him see you sweat. Champions don't let fear parade their countenance.

Fear Paralyzes

It causes immobilization. *For God has not given us a spirit of fear, but of power and of love and of a sound mind (II Timothy 1:7)*. Champions don't punk out. A punk is a worthless person, without validity, ground, merit, or a connection. Also a punk is passive and inexperienced. Punks break the law. They don't tithe and they don't love their neighbor. In a losing world, champions win. In a doubting world, champions believe God. In a slow world, champions speed up. No matter how hard it gets, champions don't punk out! Fear paralyzes by causing a person to be stuck. You have the gift and the ability, but you won't step out. You can bake cookies like Mrs. Fields, but you are afraid to start your own business.

Fear will always keep you outside of the mainstream. You feel like everybody is being blessed, but you. Don't allow fear to cause you to bail out. Grab hold to faith.

Now that you know who you are, and whose you are, it's time to walk in destiny. No longer can you stand in the shadows of your past. It's time to make your indelible impression on this earth. CHAMPION LETS GET READY TO RUMBLE!!

Prayers & Confessions

I decree and declare that I am a champion.

I fight the good fight of faith.

I win over the attacks of Satan with unwavering stamina and great perseverance.

I am a warrior who upholds and defends the integrity of God's word.

Father, I thank you that you have called me to be a champion.

Father, I thank you that you have called me to enter the ring.

Father, I thank you that you've placed upon me supernatural strength and caused my feet to be like hinds' feet.

I confess that I am victorious. I'm a conqueror. I've already won!

In Jesus' Name!

About the Author

Pastor Travis C. Jennings is an end-time prophet speaking from the heart of God. He has been commissioned to "Gather the End-Time Harvest," and is an anointed and powerful teacher of the Word of God. He is the founder and pastor of The Harvest Tabernacle Church located in Lithonia, GA. He is married to Evangelist Stephanie Jennings; the couple has four children.

www.ingramcontent.com/pod-product-compliance
Lightning Source LLC
Chambersburg PA
CBHW070646300426
44111CB00013B/2291